FIND YOUR PURPOSE

The *Destiny Talks* Workbook

JANICE GREGORY

Find Your Purpose
The Destiny Talks Workbook

All rights reserved. No part of this publication may be reproduced, distributed, or transmitted in any form or by any means, without the prior written permission of the publisher, except in the case of brief quotations embodied in critical reviews and certain other noncommercial uses permitted by copyright law.

The resources in this workbook are provided for informational purposes only and should not be used to replace the specialized training and professional judgment of a health care or mental health professional. Please always consult a trained professional before making any decision regarding treatment of yourself or others.

ISBN: 978-1-951029-27-2

Published by Wandering Words Media

©2022 Janice Gregory

To you, my fellow traveler

May your destiny shine
As brightly as
Your awesome soul!

Contents

Welcome! IX
    How to Use This Workbook IX
    Destiny Circles X

Workbook Exercises

The Journey 1
Portal I to the Soul 11
    Your Lineage
Exploring the Unknown 17
    Metaphysical Notes
Portal II to the Soul 25
    Metaphysical Tools, Part 1
Portal II to the Soul 35
    Metaphysical Tools, Part 2
Portal III to the Soul 43
    Your Life Experiences
Islands to Explore 49
    Work and Love, Part 1
Islands to Explore 57
    Work and Love, Part 2
Guiding Your Journey 65
    Navigational Tools
Guiding Your Journey 75
    Navigational Tools Encore
Skirting Treacherous Shoals, Part 1 85
Skirting Treacherous Shoals, Part 2 93
Electricity to Juice Your Navigational Tools 101
Let Your Soul and Spirit Direct Your Destiny 109
Extra Journal Pages 119
About the Author 131

Destiny Talks

"Twenty years from now you'll be more disappointed by
the things you didn't do than the ones you did do. So,
throw off the bowlines. Sail away from the safe harbor.
Catch the trade winds in your sails.
Explore. Dream. Discover."

H. Jackson Brown, Jr.

WELCOME!

> "What lies behind you and what lies in front of you,
> pales in comparison to what lies inside of you."
>
> Ralph Waldo Emerson

I'm so glad you are here!! This is the place to record your soul's journey as you choose the destiny that you desire. Let it be the very best destiny you can imagine, one that honors the essence of who you are.

Find Your Purpose: The Destiny Talks Workbook is a place to note your insights and thoughts, a workbook that you can return to time and again as you grow in self-knowledge. By writing answers to the prompts for each chapter in the book and doing the self-discovery exercises, you will delve deeper and deeper into understanding your many facets. When you reread your entries, you can reflect on what you've learned for even greater wisdom.

Practically, the workbook enables you to use the tools in *Destiny Talks: The Ultimate Guide to Connecting to Your Purpose*. It will also come in handy if you decide to work with a partner or create a Destiny Circle.

The Workbook Companion differs from the free, downloadable *Destiny Journal* in that it provides guidance from *Destiny Talks*, additional prompts, self-discovery exercises, affirmations, and meditations.

How to Use This Workbook

Use this workbook as your soul and spirit direct. This is your workbook. There are no rules except those that you set.

You don't have to write out answers to the questions. You can, for example, take notes, use bullet points, draw pictures, doodle (which lets your subconscious direct your answers), or just contemplate your answers. If you need more space, there are extra pages at the end of the workbook.

You also can choose which prompts to respond to and which exercises to do. Choose whatever appeals to you. Skip what doesn't.

Destiny Circles

A profound joy lies in deeply connecting with others as you progress on your journey of self-discovery and direct your destiny. As well as using the workbook on its own, you can use it to spark conversations with a partner or as a basis for conversations with a Destiny Circle consisting of three or more members.

There is no set curriculum for a Destiny Circle. You can tackle as few or as many subjects from *Destiny Talks* as your members choose.

I recommend that your Destiny Circle meet once a week for sixty to ninety minutes to discuss each of the book's topics. I like to spend at least two meetings on each subject. At the first meeting, members discuss what they know about the topic and where members can find out more information to aid in their quest. At the subsequent meeting, three or more members spend twenty minutes each sharing what they have found out about themselves. Other members listen attentively and provide positive insights.

Alternatively, you could hold longer meetings once a month. You can also take weeks off to undertake self-discovery exercises on your own or with Destiny Circle members. The choice for how long and often you schedule your meetings depends on your members' preferences.

Like many book clubs, a Destiny Circle can have a social aspect where members catch up over coffee and snacks. How wonderful it will be to learn more about the soul mates in your circle.

Self-Discovery Exercises

Self-discovery exercises are included in each chapter of the workbook. Designed to be joyful experiences, the activities will lead you on a metaphorical treasure hunt to discover your authentic self.

You might want to undertake the exercises with a partner or a member of your Destiny Circle. Be sure to schedule enough time to both do the exercise and analyze its meaning. You don't need to write everything down. You can just discuss your discoveries with a friend.

Affirmations

Developing a daily practice of speaking affirmations morning and night can amplify how much you enjoy your journey of self-discovery. I provide examples of affirmations at the end of each chapter. I encourage you to create your own.

Let me take a moment here to explain what affirmations are and how to create effective ones.

According to Jack Canfield, *New York Times* bestselling author of *The Success Principle: How to Get from Where You Are to Where You Want to Be*, affirmations are:

> …simple positive statements declaring specific goals in their completed states. Although they sound rather basic at that level, these empowering mantras have profound effects on the conscious and unconscious mind.

Canfield lists eight guidelines for creating mantras:

1. Start with the words, "I am." These are the two most powerful words in the English language.
2. Use the present tense.
3. State it in the positive. Affirm what you want, not what you don't want.
4. Keep it brief.
5. Be specific.
6. Include an action word ending in "-ing."
7. Include at least one dynamic emotion or feeling word.
8. Make affirmations for yourself, not others.[1]

Here are some examples:

> I am relaxing in my beautiful villa overlooking the Mediterranean Sea.
>
> I am doing a happy dance as I realize that my life is filled with love and friendship.
>
> I am joyously basking in thunderous applause as I receive an award for my humanitarian service.

Notice that each affirmation doesn't necessarily follow all of Canfield's recommendations. However, they generally capture the uplifting emotion of an enjoyable event occurring to you in the present time.

Canfield gives a simple formula for creating an affirmation. Just complete the sentence, "I am so happy and grateful that I am now…"

The point of affirmations in this workbook is to make you feel good about the unique desires of your soul and counter any negative self-talk that may limit your progress. It should also help you realize your fondest dreams, which, with a little help from the Divine, can help you create your destiny.

---

[1] Canfield, Jack. "Daily Affirmations for Positive Thinking." https://www.jackcanfield.com/blog/practice-daily-affirmations/.

MEDITATIONS

After the affirmations, I suggest a thought or topic for you to meditate on. I may ask a question for you to ponder. Sometimes, I will suggest that you meditate on an affirmation. This is a lovely way to raise your vibration and make your dreams come true.

I use the terms, "meditate" and "meditation," loosely. There are many prescribed meditation methods. I suggest that, after all your work, you simply contemplate or meditate on your findings. You can do this by sitting still, centering yourself with your breath, clearing your mind, and seeing what comes to you. You can also meditate by going for a walk, journaling, or thinking about what you've written and the exercises you've undertaken.

You might just read the meditative thought or question a couple of times and consider it as you go about your day. You never know how an insight will come to you. Many of us get our best ideas while we are showering, exercising, or sleeping. We aren't consciously focused on our question, but our souls and brains are noodling away in the background. They will shoot us an "aha" moment from out of the blue.

The goal is to give yourself time to integrate what you've learned before moving on to the next subject. For example, at the beginning of a chapter, you may consider your greatest desire to be for unbridled wealth. By the time you've answered the questions and meditated, you may realize that what you really want is the time and freedom that money buys. This leads you to ask further what you would do with more time and freedom. By going deeper with your questions, answers, and meditations, you will discover your soul's desires and a pathway to realizing your unique destiny.

Remember that self-realization is a lifetime journey. Don't feel that you have to answer every question and do every exercise to know who you are and become who you'd like to be. Imagine that you are choosing delicacies at a sumptuous banquet. Let delight be your guide as you choose which enticing foods to put on your plate.

Let's begin!

THE JOURNEY

"Self-knowledge is the pathway to the soul. So,
take me down deep, Lord, and reveal to me my true self."

Caroline Myss

THE JOURNEY

We are all on a life journey. How we give voice to our soul and spirit through our words and actions determines the unique character of our journey—our destiny. Our own reactions to life's challenges and joys determine the meaning of our lives. Combined with the rest of humanity's choices, it shapes Earth's destiny.

Seen in this light, our decisions, as we create our destiny, are immensely important. They can lift humankind up or drag it down.

Your answers to the prompts in this section will record where you are in your journey now. You might start your record by free writing for ten to fifteen minutes on what you know for sure about yourself so far and what you look forward to exploring in the future. Free writing is writing continuously without lifting your pen or stopping to edit what you have written. It's a great way to access your subconscious thoughts.

You could also journal or free write your answers to any or all of the following questions. Choose whatever intuitively appeals to you. Skip what doesn't.

Remember, there are extra pages at the end of this workbook if you don't have enough room to write your answers under a question.

JOURNAL PROMPTS

1. *Destiny Talks* begins with the poem, *Ithaka,* by Constantine Cavafy. What does this poem mean to you? If it didn't resonate with you, note that here. We'll revisit the poem at the end of the book.

2. Where are you in the process of self-discovery? What is driving you forward?

3. What life obstacles have you overcome? What are the personal strengths and skills that have enabled your success?

4. What portal(s) in *Destiny Talks* are you drawn to explore: your lineage, the metaphysical, and/or your life experiences? Why?

_____
_____
_____
_____
_____
_____
_____
_____
_____
_____
_____
_____
_____
_____
_____
_____
_____
_____

5. Is there anyone you would like to bring with you on your journey? How will you invite others to participate?

SELF-DISCOVERY EXERCISE

Create a vision board which depicts your vision of Ithaka. To do this, you might contemplate your answers to the following questions:
- o Where would you like to arrive at your journey's end?
- o What would your ideal destination look like?
- o What would you have accomplished?
- o What would your life look like?

Here are basic suggestions for how to create a vision board:

1. In the center of a white poster board, sketch pad, or a regular piece of paper, draw a circle. In the center of the circle, draw a representation of the divinity that is going to help direct your journey. You could draw angels, a big "S" for spirit, a picture or representation of God—whatever force you believe has your back.
2. Now consider the categories of life that you care about, such as family, friends, pets, health, love life, career/calling, self-development/education, wealth or abundance, living or home environment, passions/hobbies, or charities or causes. Paste or draw pictures of your ideal life as it relates to some or all of these categories outside of the circle on your board.

This is a very basic vision board based on Colette Baron-Reid's work. You can learn more about how to construct vision boards by Googling vision boards online. Also, there are free online apps which will help you create a digital vision board, including Dream Vision Board, Hay House Vision Board, and My Vision Board.

AFFIRMATIONS

My heart overflows with gratitude for the delightful life I am living.

On my wondrous journey, I am discovering my magical self.

Your affirmation:

_____

_____

_____

_____

_____

_____

_____

MEDITATION

What does your Ithaka look like? Can you imagine how you will feel when you are living your purpose and are on a journey to fulfilling your dreams?

_____

_____

_____

_____

_____

_____

PORTAL I TO THE SOUL

YOUR LINEAGE

"Carve your name on hearts, not tombstones.
A legacy is etched into the minds of others
and the stories they share about you."

Shannon L. Alder

Portal I to the Soul: Your Lineage

One of the ways to understand who you are is to explore your relationship with relatives and ancestors. Knowing who they are, or were, will provide insight into your nature. You may have inherited certain traits. You may have also learned behaviors from family members' examples. Once you understand your traits and behaviors, you can choose which to enhance and which to jettison.

Journal Prompts

1. Who in your extended family fascinates you? What characteristics and personal gifts do you share?

___
___
___
___
___
___
___
___
___
___

2. Does a mystery surround a family member? What qualities and/or stories about this family member intrigue you?

SELF-DISCOVERY EXERCISES

Talk to your friends and family about your family lineage, especially people who you are curious about. What insights do they offer?

___
___
___
___
___
___
___
___
___
___
___
___
___
___
___
___
___
___
___

Where can you find more information about your lineage and the family members who inspire you? If you want to learn more about a person, brainstorm three actions you can take to indulge your curiosity. Set a date for taking action. If you need help figuring out where to find information, ask a librarian, friends, or a member of a genealogical society. You might want to undertake this activity with a friend or Destiny Circle member.

_____

_____

_____

_____

_____

_____

_____

_____

_____

_____

_____

_____

_____

_____

_____

AFFIRMATIONS

I am successfully creating a positive legacy for my family.

I am so pleased to discover the outstanding personal qualities of my family and our lineage.

Your affirmation:

_____
_____
_____
_____
_____
_____

MEDITATION

What are your superpowers? Meditate on a personal strength you share with your relatives.

_____
_____
_____
_____
_____
_____

Exploring the Unknown

Metaphysical Notes

"There are more things in Heaven and Earth, Horatio,
than are dreamt of in your philosophy."

William Shakespeare

Exploring the Unknown Metaphysical Notes

Meta means beyond or transcending. Metaphysics refers to the study of phenomena that cannot be observed, events that transcend the physical. It is a branch of philosophy derived from Plato's belief that what exists lies beyond experience.

Metaphysical tools, such as astrology, oracle cards, past life regression, and numerology, can be delightful aides for gaining insight into your soul's purpose. Since metaphysics is based on the unobservable, you will need to use your judgment to determine if your insights ring true.

Journal Prompts

1. Are you drawn to metaphysics? If yes, which subjects pique your curiosity? Which ones have you explored? Which would you like to study?

_____
_____
_____
_____
_____
_____
_____
_____
_____

2. If you are skeptical about metaphysics, why do you doubt its usefulness?

3. How does your intuition speak to you? Does it speak to you through one of your five senses, or does it have some other way of grabbing your attention?

4. When has your intuition led you to positive experiences and/or kept you from danger?

SELF-DISCOVERY EXERCISES

Pay close attention to your intuition over the course of the next week. Note when your intuition gives you information ahead of events or knowledge about an event or person. For example, does someone you have been thinking about text or call you unexpectedly? Can you predict how someone will react to an email you sent?

_____
_____
_____
_____
_____
_____
_____
_____
_____
_____
_____
_____
_____
_____
_____
_____
_____

Become aware of how your senses—smelling a pleasant/unpleasant odor, reading a passage that answers a question in the back of your mind, hearing lyrics that uplift you—rather than your logic, provide insight into your feelings

AFFIRMATIONS

My intuition is creating an outstanding life with me.

I am gladly reading Divine signs that lead me in the direction of my highest good.

Your affirmation:

_____

_____

_____

_____

_____

_____

MEDITATION

Set an intention to learn what is in your highest good to know. Clear your mind of conscious thoughts and sit quietly for the next fifteen to twenty minutes. See what images or thoughts come to you. Know that you might not receive guidance as you meditate, but you might receive guiding signs over the next couple of days. What images and insights come to you?

_____

_____

_____

_____

_____

Portal II to the Soul

Metaphysical Tools, Part 1

"There's a divinity that shapes our ends,
rough-hew them how we will."

William Shakespeare

Portal II to the Soul
Metaphysical Tools, Part 1

Astrology

You can obtain a free birth chart which shows where the astrological signs were at the date, time, and location of your birth by going to www.astro.com, or you can Google free astrological charts and check out other sites.

Here are the *basic* positive energies for the astrological signs:

>   Aries—bold, action-oriented, leader
>   Taurus—dependable, solidly grounded, sensual
>   Gemini—fast-moving, quick-thinking, talkative
>   Cancer—empathetic, sensitive, adaptable
>   Leo—dramatic, self-confident, fun
>   Virgo—organized, detail-oriented, practical
>   Libra—balanced, social, idealistic
>   Scorpio—mysterious, intense, persevering
>   Sagittarius—independent, adventurous, enthusiastic
>   Capricorn—achieving, driven, ambitious
>   Aquarius—innovative, eccentric, future-oriented
>   Pisces—intuitive, idealistic, kind

Each of the signs can be described with other adjectives and have shadow or dark aspects as well. Feel free to use what you know from other sources to describe the energies of the signs in answering the journal prompts.

Journal Prompts

1. Fill in each blank with the appropriate sign from your birth chart:

    Your sun sign_____

    Your ascendant (rising) sign_____

Your moon sign_____

The sign at your midheaven_____

2. What characteristics of your sun and ascendant signs describe you? Do their energies reinforce each other or clash?

_____

_____

_____

_____

_____

_____

_____

_____

_____

_____

_____

_____

_____

_____

_____

3. How do the characteristics of your moon sign influence your actions?

4. What is the energy from the sign at your midheaven that is affecting your career path?

NUMEROLOGY

According to numerologists, numbers have specific energies. The following are the *basic* positive and negative energies of the numbers one through nine:

    1—leader, spirited, initiating, self-centered
    2—partner, sensitive, supportive, passive, self-sacrificing
    3—joyous, exuberant, optimistic, scattered, unpredictable
    4—hardworking, disciplined, systematic, rigid, demanding
    5—impulsive, adventurous, energetic, unfocused, chaotic
    6—loving, responsible, a time of marriage or divorce, martyr
    7—mystical, scientific, introverted, solitary, aloof
    8—powerful, achiever, money-making, materialistic
    9—transforming, completing, serving mankind, challenging

Understanding numerology is more than just knowing the energies of the first nine numbers. There are also master and karmic numbers, several ways to combine numbers to create new meanings, and different ways to apply numbers to understand distinct time periods in your life. Still, you can glean some fundamental ideas about the energy in your name and birth date from the description of the numbers above.

In order to interpret the energy in your name, you will need to change letters to numbers. The letters in the alphabet translate into the following numbers:

    A,J,S=1   B,K,T=2   C,L,U=3   D,M,V=4
    E,N,W=5   F,O,X=6   G,P,Y=7   H,Q,Z=8
    I,R,=9

1. What is your destiny number? _____

This is the reduced sum of the numbers in your birth name as written on your birth certificate. Use the chart on the previous page to change the letters in your name to numbers. Add the numbers, then reduce to a single digit.

Here is an example of how to do this. Oprah Winfrey's birth name is Orpah Gail Winfrey. It's Orpah, not Oprah, on her birth certificate. She was named after a Biblical character in the *Book of Ruth*. If you substitute numbers for letters, her name translates to 6+9+7+1+8=31 for Orpah, 7+1+9+3=20 for Gail, and 5+9+5+6+9+5+7=46 for Winfrey.

Oprah's three names reduce to the numbers 31, 20, and 46, which can be added together and further reduced as (3+1) + (2+0) + (4+6) =16, and then finally reduced by adding 1+6=7. Oprah's destiny number is 7, the number of a spiritual leader.

_____

_____

_____

_____

2. What is your life path number? _____

This is the reduced sum of the numbers of your birth date. For example, you can write December 1, 1976, as 12/01/1976. You can then add the numbers in this date as follows, (1+2) + (0+1) + (1+9+7+6) =27. You can reduce 27 further by adding 2+7=9. Nine, which is the number of a humanitarian, is the reduced life path number for December 1, 1976.

_____

_____

_____

_____

3. What is the number of your soul's purpose or heart's desire? _____

The reduced sum of the number of the vowels in your name indicates your soul's purpose or heart's desire.

Again, using Oprah as an example, her name contains the following vowels. Orpah has the vowels "o" and "a," Gail has "a" and "i," and Winfrey has "i" and "e." According to our chart, o=6, a=1, i=9, and e=5. The sum of the vowels in Oprah's birth name are (6+1) + (1+9) + (9+5), which equals (7) + (10) + (14) =31. 31 can be reduced by adding 3+1 together, which equals 4. Oprah values hard work and creating practical, systematic solutions to problems.

_____
_____
_____
_____
_____
_____

4. What is your realization number? _____

This number is determined by adding your destiny and life path numbers together and reducing the answer to one digit.

The realization number describes the energy that will influence the second half of your life, that is, from around the age of fifty onward.

_____
_____
_____
_____
_____
_____

5. Free write or journal on what your astrological signs and numbers say about your personality, life path, and destiny.

_____

_____

_____

_____

_____

SELF-DISCOVERY EXERCISES

Research more information on astrology and numerology on the internet or in books. You can obtain a list of references from my website, www.janicegregory.com.

The Idiot's Guide to Astrology by Madeline Gerwick-Brodeur and Lisa Lenard as well as *The Idiot's Guide to Numerology* by Kay Lagerquist and Lisa Lenard provide excellent introductory material on astrology and numerology.

There are countless other books and websites on astrology. I've found Debra Silverman's website, www.debrasilvermanastrology.com, and her social media posts illuminating and fun.

In terms of numerology, I'd recommend Carol Adrienne, www.caroladrienne.com, who wrote *The Purpose of Your Life.* As the title indicates, her book applies numerology to understanding your life purpose.

Michelle Buchanan, www.michellebuchanan.co.nz, in her book, *The Numerology Guidebook: Uncover Your Destiny and the Blueprint of Your Life,* also provides clear explanations of how to unlock numerology's wisdom.

Share your findings with a friend or members of your Destiny Circle.

AFFIRMATIONS

I delight in discovering that my perfect destiny is described by the alignment of the stars at my birth.

The numerological energy from my name, combined with the stars' alignment, has predicted my unique and wonderful personality.

Your affirmation:

_____

_____

_____

_____

_____

_____

MEDITATION

Meditate on your stellar and unique qualities.

_____

_____

_____

_____

_____

_____

Portal II to the Soul

Metaphysical Tools, Part 2

"It is never too late to be what you might have been."

George Eliot

Portal II to the Soul
Metaphysical Tools, Part 2

I've gained meaningful insights about my life's trajectory from meeting with psychics/mediums. My sessions have not been so much about predicting the future as about understanding my past, particularly my relationships and how these have and continue to influence my life choices—past, present, and future. By understanding the forces working behind me, perhaps in the ether, I can make more conscious choices in the present. Those choices will, of course, influence my future. A key variable in this equation is finding the right psychic/medium, one who speaks with integrity and compassion.

Exploring your past lives through past life therapy or regression analysis can also provide healing insights into your present circumstances and, thus, a way to consciously affect your destiny. The healer, in this case, hypnotizes the client by putting them into a deeply relaxed state. Through guided meditation, the healer leads the client back into past lives to uncover experiences that profoundly impact their present life.

Journal Prompts

1. What life or relationship issues challenge you? How?

_____

_____

_____

_____

_____

_____

_____

_____

2. What have you found helpful in guiding your understanding of the challenges?

3. Have you ever gone to a reader or psychic/medium? What were the circumstances? What did you learn about yourself?

4. If you haven't looked into working with a psychic/medium or a therapist who offers past life regression sessions, what has kept you from doing so? Are there particular types of readings you are interested in? Why or why not?

___

SELF-DISCOVERY EXERCISES

Seek out a trusted healer to work with. Word-of-mouth may be the best way to get a referral in your area. Consult with friends about their experiences. Take your time so that you find someone who is legitimate and whose style appeals to you. You can also look up healers that I reference in my book or on my website, www.janicegregory.com. However, the demand for these individual's services has become so great that many of them have given up private practice to reach a wider audience through writing and teaching.

Online courses, including ones taught by Dr. Brian Weiss and Sandra Anne Taylor, can help you access the power of past life regression therapy and the Akashic Records. Just Google their names to find the appropriate websites and their offerings.

Discuss with a friend or Destiny Circle member what you have learned from your research and in-person readings. Take notes on significant insights.

_____

_____

_____

_____

_____

_____

_____

_____

_____

_____

_____

_____

_____

Affirmations

I am growing wiser and more compassionate as I learn about my life challenges.

My journey of self-discovery has revealed that I'm a wondrously unique and gifted person.

Your affirmation:

_____

_____

_____

_____

_____

Meditation

Meditate on a happy insight you've gained on your journey and/or an affirmation that appeals to you.

_____

_____

_____

_____

_____

_____

Portal III to the Soul

Your Life Experiences

"The imagination is literally the workshop wherein
are fashioned all plans created by man."

Napoleon Hill

Portal III to the Soul
Your Life Experiences

You don't need astrologists, numerologists, or tarot card readers to understand your destiny. An equally valid way is to dig into understanding your life on your own, or with the help of friends, family, and/or a counselor.

Journal Prompts

1. As you consider your life, what kinds of experiences would you like to create more of? What kinds of experiences would you like to eliminate from your future life? How might you accomplish these changes?

___
___
___
___
___
___
___
___
___
___

2. Who are the five most influential people in your life today? What do you value about them and your relationship with them? What qualities do they possess that reflect aspects of yourself?

SELF-DISCOVERY EXERCISES

Create something that depicts your life so far. Then add to your creation or create another piece which illustrates how you would like your future life to look. Your creative project can include drawings, writing, music, dance, or whatever spurs your imagination. What insights do you gain about your life and future?

___

Try meditating, free-writing, drawing, reading, or another creative activity each day at the same time for a week. Evaluate the experience. Decide if you'd like to continue with the practice and make it into a habit. Creating a habit takes approximately twenty-one days of consistent practice.

Affirmations

I am inspired by my life and relationships every day.

My life is a marvelous, creative work of art.

Your affirmation:

_____

_____

_____

_____

_____

_____

Meditation

Meditate on an event, person, or thought that lifts your spirits.

_____

_____

_____

_____

_____

_____

ISLANDS TO EXPLORE

WORK AND LOVE, PART I

"You are what your deep, driving desire is.
As your desire is, so is your will.
As your will is, so is your deed.
As your deed is, so is your destiny."

Brihadaranyaka Upanishad IV.4.5

ISLANDS TO EXPLORE
WORK AND LOVE, PART I

How you interact with your work environment speaks volumes about you. It includes a myriad of complex relationships—bosses, colleagues, customers, employees, and others—for you to navigate. The physical environment—whether a home office, a manufacturing facility, or an office building—and commuting present another set of issues. Then, of course, there's the ultimate challenge: managing work-life balance.

Juggling all the demands is seldom easy. It's almost always a work-in-progress.

JOURNAL PROMPTS

1. Assess your work environment. What/who is supporting you? What stresses you out?

2. What role do you play in creating your successes and challenges?

3. How can you change your environment to make it more supportive? If you can't change your circumstances, can you change your beliefs about it so that you feel happier?

4. How can you claim your power and show up authentically? What might be the risks and rewards of doing so?

SELF-DISCOVERY EXERCISE

At the beginning and end of each day for the next three weeks, think of someone or something you are grateful for in your work environment. Keep track of these items here or in a gratitude notebook.

Remember the aphorism, "What you appreciate, appreciates." It grows in both size and value. The people and experiences you consistently value in your life will appreciate with your focused gratitude.

_____

_____

_____

_____

_____

_____

_____

_____

_____

_____

_____

_____

_____

_____

_____

AFFIRMATIONS

I am loving my work as I receive high praise for my accomplishments from all around me.

I inspire my mentors and colleagues who help me to flourish.

Your affirmation:

_____

_____

_____

_____

_____

_____

_____

_____

_____

_____

_____

_____

_____

Meditation

What does your perfect work environment look and feel like? How do you interact with your colleagues, supervisor(s), and/or employees in this environment? What is your ideal work environment? Even if you don't know the answer to these questions, imagine how you would feel if you were using your unique gifts in a job you loved.

_____

_____

_____

_____

_____

_____

_____

_____

Islands to Explore

Work and Love, Part 2

"Let yourself be silently drawn by the strange pull of what you really love. It will not lead you astray."

Rumi

Islands to Explore
Work and Love, Part 2

Our mettle is determined in the arenas of relationships and love. They can provoke the most tender, generous actions, and they can make us into monsters exacting untold destruction.

Here is where self-knowledge, control, and conscious decision-making can determine our destiny. We have choice; free will is ours. We can reflect on a situation or relationship and decide how to act. We can seek revenge or turn the other cheek.

Journal Prompts

1. Reflect on your love affairs and friendships. How have you enhanced the quality of experiences with people you love?

___

___

___

___

___

___

___

___

___

2. What could you do differently to build stronger relationships? What would be the consequences for your life if you created better relationships?

SELF-DISCOVERY EXERCISES

List the most significant relationships in your life, then group them into categories: family, friends, romantic partners, bosses, colleagues, or mentors, for example. You don't need to fill in all of the categories, and you can add different ones. If someone fits into two or more categories, put them into the one that seems the most apt.

_____
_____
_____
_____
_____
_____
_____
_____
_____
_____
_____
_____
_____
_____
_____
_____
_____

Now list the primary characteristics—kind, fun, critical, sensitive, abusive, etc.—of the people in each of these categories.

Analyze what these relationships say about you, your values, and your mode of interacting with others. Which relationships would you like to enhance, and which do you need to limit? How will you accomplish this?

___

___

___

___

___

___

___

___

___

___

___

___

___

___

___

___

___

___

___

___

Affirmations

My relationships are nourishing, supportive, and uplifting.

My days are filled with friendship, laughter, and deep meaning.

Your affirmation:

___

Meditation

Meditate on cherished characteristics of your loved ones.

___

Guiding Your Journey

Navigational Tools

"Whenever you are faced with a choice, a decision, or an opportunity, choose in favor of your passions."

Janet Bray Attwood and Chris Attwood

GUIDING YOUR JOURNEY NAVIGATIONAL TOOLS

A vast amount of research shows that it's not success that leads to happiness; rather, happiness causes success. Be happy first, and you will achieve much more than if you are low-spirited.

If you want to inject happiness throughout your life, you need to first figure out what brings you joy. Then let joy guide your course. Finally, to sustain your sense of well-being, you must be open to new experiences. Be flexible. Don't be overly attached to the outcome of your efforts.

You may not reach the goal, or destination, that you fervently desired. Destiny may send winds that blow you in another, perhaps a better direction. The challenge is to look for the meaning in your experiences and ultimately to find the joy in your journey.

JOURNAL PROMPTS

1. What/who has brought you sustained happiness? Why?

_____
_____
_____
_____
_____
_____
_____
_____
_____

2. Have you ever set a goal and achieved it? How did you feel immediately, and then six months later? What have been the long-term outcomes of your success? Did it set you on a path that you never imagined?

_____

3. Are you living a passion-filled life? Do you really want to be happier? What might be the consequences of becoming happier?

4. What do you dream of achieving in your life? What goals might help you realize your dreams?

5. How committed are you to working on your goals? Can you hand over your concerns about the results to the Divine?

___

SELF-DISCOVERY EXERCISES:

Complete the sentence, "When my life is ideal, I am…"[2]

> List as many activities and circumstances as you'd like. Examples might include, "I am connecting joyfully with friends and family members," "I am living peacefully in a house overlooking the sea," or "I radiate good health as I dance the night away."
>
> These, of course, are affirmations. You are claiming your ideal life for the present.

___

___

___

___

___

___

___

___

___

___

___

___

___

___

___

___

___

---

[2] Janet Bray Attwood and Chris Attwood. *The Passion Test: The Effortless Path to Discovering Your Life Purpose* (New York: Penguin Group, 2008), 30.

Return to these affirmations in a few months' time. How many of them already describe your life?

Affirmations

I am amazed at how I'm living the life of my fondest dreams.

The Divine is helping me create a more enriched and splendid life than I could possibly have imagined.

Your affirmation:

_____

_____

_____

_____

_____

_____

Meditation

Meditate on your ideal life. Where are you? What are you doing? What emotions are you feeling?

_____

_____

_____

_____

_____

_____

Guiding Your Journey

Navigational Tools Encore

"At times you have to leave the city of your comfort and go into the wilderness of your intuition. What you'll discover will be wonderful. What you'll discover is yourself."

Alan Alda

Guiding Your Journey
Navigational Tools Encore

In addition to using your passions as a GPS, you can use your intuition to build a fulfilling life. This is a practiced skill that comes much easier to some than to others. In general, your intuition talks to you through your other five senses.

Other tools for understanding and then guiding your life's trajectory are meditation, consulting with oracle or tarot cards, using creative visualization, raising your vibrational frequency, and employing affirmations.

Journal Prompts

1. What are the primary and secondary ways that your intuition speaks to you? Hearing, sight, feelings, smell, taste, or a sense of just knowing?

_____
_____
_____
_____
_____
_____
_____
_____
_____
_____

2. When has your intuition revealed a truth or future event to you?

3. Are you willing to let your intuition guide your life? Why or why not?

4. Have you ever had a card reading? What did you learn from the reading? Was it helpful or not? Why?

5. Have you had any experience with trying to manifest an event through creative visualization or the Law of Attraction? What was the outcome? Why do you think this was?

___
___
___
___
___
___
___
___
___
___
___
___
___
___
___
___
___
___
___
___

SELF-DISCOVERY EXERCISES

Go for an oracle or tarot card reading. What was the experience like? What did you find out about yourself?

Make a list of things you'd like to do and people you'd like to talk with. This could be as simple as going on a walk to a new place or emailing a friend you've lost contact with. You could visit a museum, garden, or a park you've never visited. Find an activity that you anticipate with joy and see what comes from your adventure.

AFFIRMATIONS

I am discovering new ways to bring joy into my life.

Wondrous new adventures and relationships are enriching my days.

Your affirmation:

_____

_____

_____

_____

_____

MEDITATION

Set an intention to learn more about what makes you happy. Clear your mind, meditate, and see what comes up.

For the next week or so, notice when you are feeling happy. Jot down your findings here. Contemplate what these findings mean for your life going forward.

_____

_____

_____

_____

_____

Skirting Treacherous Shoals, Part 1

"The cave you fear to enter is where your power lies."

Joseph Campbell

SKIRTING TREACHEROUS SHOALS, PART 1

Your demons lurk in darkness, ever ready to sabotage your trip. The worst among these are self-criticism and a lack of self-confidence. They can deep-six your best efforts.

If you lack self-confidence, you might turn your ship around, or worse yet, abandon it altogether. Yet if you can build your confidence, your journey's success is almost assured. You will know abundant riches, a treasure chest filled with emeralds, rubies, sapphires, and diamonds.

There is no surefire way to accomplish this, but if you are committed to cherishing your very soul, there are lots of tools to aid in your endeavors. You will need to return to these tools time and again. Turning your ship around from low to high self-confidence is not for the faint-hearted. It takes dedication.

JOURNAL PROMPTS

1. List all your limiting beliefs without editing. Then identify the top three to five beliefs that hold you back the most.

_____
_____
_____
_____
_____
_____
_____
_____

2. Can you identify where these beliefs came from? How old were you when you started believing each one?

3. What is your relationship to money? Does money come easily to you? Do you feel comfortable with how much you save, spend, and give away?

4. What money beliefs influence your earning and spending patterns? For example, do you believe that money doesn't grow on trees or that rich people are greedy? What effects have these beliefs had on how much money you have and how you use it? Can you turn any of these beliefs around to your advantage?

SELF-DISCOVERY EXERCISES

Examine your limiting life and money beliefs. Can you be sure that each belief is true? What makes you think so? Use Byron Katie's questions from The Work, www.thework.com, to turn your beliefs around. Alternatively, reframe your beliefs to create more positive statements that will encourage your success.

_____

_____

_____

_____

_____

_____

_____

_____

_____

_____

_____

_____

_____

_____

_____

_____

One of the ways we undermine our self-confidence is through negative self-talk. Many of us have an inner voice that constantly talks to us. It can undermine our self-confidence if it continually criticizes our decisions and actions.

> Note here what your inner voice says to you over the coming days. Whenever you hear it speak negatively to you, change its narrative. For example, it might say, "You're such a fool for overloading your schedule." You should immediately correct it by saying, "I am smart for creating a productive schedule. All is working out for the best." See how often your positive statements come true.

_____

_____

_____

_____

_____

_____

_____

_____

_____

_____

_____

_____

Affirmations

I easily set and accomplish my goals.

Money loves me. It comes to me easily in unexpected and pleasant surprises.

Your affirmation:

_____

_____

_____

_____

_____

_____

Meditation

Meditate on what abundance means to you.

_____

_____

_____

_____

_____

_____

_____

SKIRTING TREACHEROUS SHOALS, PART 2

"If you do not change your direction,
you may end up where you are heading."

Lao Tzu

Skirting Treacherous Shoals, Part 2

Other tools, such as creative visualization, affirmations, mirror work, and Emotional Freedom Technique (EFT)/tapping, can effectively counteract the sabotaging force of negative beliefs.

Journal Prompts

1. At this point, you should have some idea about what lights you up and what you long to accomplish in this life. What is holding you back from living a passionate life and realizing your dreams?

_____
_____
_____
_____
_____
_____
_____
_____
_____
_____
_____
_____

2. Reflect on the negative beliefs you identified in the previous chapter. Which ones still weigh you down?

3. Which modalities—creative visualization, affirmations, mirror work, and/or EFT—can you use to counteract your doubts? Are there other ways you can increase your self-confidence?

SELF-DISCOVERY EXERCISES

Develop a routine that incorporates one or more of these techniques into your daily living for the next twenty-one days. Research indicates that if you take consistent action over the course of three weeks, the action will become a habit. What is your new routine?

Journal at the beginning and end of undertaking a new routine or using a technique to counteract your limiting beliefs. What effect does it have on your life?

Affirmations

I am so worthy of the marvelous new life I'm creating.

I love life, and life loves me.

Your affirmation:

_____

_____

_____

_____

_____

Meditation

What do you love about yourself and your life?

_____

_____

_____

_____

_____

Electricity to Juice Your Navigational Tools

"Say yes. Whatever it is, say yes with your whole heart,
and as simple as it sounds, that's all the excuse life
needs to grab your hands and start to dance."

Brian Andreas

Electricity to Juice Your Navigational Tools

You'll need to plug into faith, detachment, gratitude, and joy to realize your chosen destiny.

Journal Prompts

1. Do you believe that you can create a fabulous destiny? What events have shown you that the Universe/Divine values your soul's desires?

_____
_____
_____
_____
_____
_____
_____
_____
_____
_____
_____
_____

2. Are you attached to how your destiny manifests? Why or why not?

3. What have you experienced that has been better than you imagined? What are some unexpected, lovely events or relationships in your life that have occurred without you seeking them out?

___

___

___

___

___

___

___

___

___

___

___

___

___

___

___

___

___

___

___

SELF-DISCOVERY EXERCISES

List people and things that you are grateful for. Include activities and people that make you smile. Whenever you are downhearted, return to this list. Are there things you could do, or people you could call, to raise your spirits?

_____
_____
_____
_____
_____
_____
_____
_____
_____
_____
_____
_____
_____
_____
_____
_____

Get together with a close friend or friends. Discuss your insights into the trajectories of your lives. What are you excited about doing now and in the future?

AFFIRMATIONS

I am profoundly grateful for the fabulous people in my life.

Miracles happen when I let go of caring about the outcomes of my good faith efforts.

Your Affirmation:

___

MEDITATION

Meditate on someone you are grateful for. What do you particularly love about them?

Let Your Soul and Spirit Direct Your Destiny

"If you have built castles in the air, your work need not be lost;
that is where they should be. Now put the foundations under them."

Henry David Thoreau

LET YOUR SOUL AND SPIRIT DIRECT YOUR DESTINY

Your soul and spirit hold your destiny. Your soul is your essence, your light. It determines what brings you joy and fulfillment. If you let your soul be your rudder, you can use it to steer you to the perfect destination.

Your spirit is the wind in your sails. If it is energized, your sails will billow. You will sail swiftly in your chosen direction. If it is dejected, you will drift listlessly, perhaps even sink, as oncoming storms batter your ship.

It is imperative that you honor your soul and spirit. Treat them as the Divine gifts they are. As you start out on your journey, you need only have faith that they are the guides to your enlightened destiny, and, indeed, to this planet's future.

JOURNAL PROMPTS

1. Reread *Ithaka,* the poem by Constantine Cavafy, at the beginning of *Destiny Talks*. What does it mean to you now? How far have you traveled?

_____

_____

_____

_____

_____

_____

_____

_____

2. Review your answers to the questions in the previous chapters. What are your most significant insights?

3. Describe the destiny you would like to create, the Ithaka you'd like to reach.

4. How can you make the journey to your destination blissful? Will you treasure its riches?

Self-Discovery Exercises

List three to five steps you can take to launch your ship toward its destiny. Once you have taken these steps, review your course and destination. Then determine additional steps you want to take.

Create your own Journey to Ithaka journal. Pick a notebook that you are comfortable writing in. Make a title page. Then on the first page draw and/or write about your Ithaka or chosen destiny. Every morning, free-write three pages on where you are, where you're headed, or whatever is on your mind. After three weeks, reread your entries. If this was a rewarding exercise, continue with it!

Affirmations

My life's journey is resplendent with love and abundance.

My soul and spirit shine ever brighter as I realize my unique beauty.

Your affirmation:

_____
_____
_____
_____
_____
_____

Meditation

Meditate on the wonderful past and future adventures in your life.

_____
_____
_____
_____
_____
_____

CONGRATULATIONS!!

Celebrate! You have taken valiant steps toward realizing your brilliant self!

Your amazing destiny awaits!

Extra Journal Pages

Find Your Purpose

Find Your Purpose

Find Your Purpose

About the Author

Janice Gregory co-authored the bestselling book, *The Happiness Code: How Small Habits Will Change Your Life Starting Today*. Her work is also featured in *The Powys Journal* in England. A certified coach, she is a numerologist, a Passion Test facilitator, and an oracle card reader. Prior to starting her coaching business, Janice was a small business consultant for twenty-five years with the University System of New Hampshire, where she designed award-winning, nationally recognized entrepreneurial programs. She earned her B.A. from Harvard College and her M.P.A. from the Harvard Kennedy School. Janice lives in Newburyport, Massachusetts. You can reach her at www.janicegregory.com.

www.ingramcontent.com/pod-product-compliance
Lightning Source LLC
Chambersburg PA
CBHW051805100526
44592CB00016B/2569